ENGINEERING CHALLENGES

BUILDING SKYSCRAPERS

by Marne Ventura

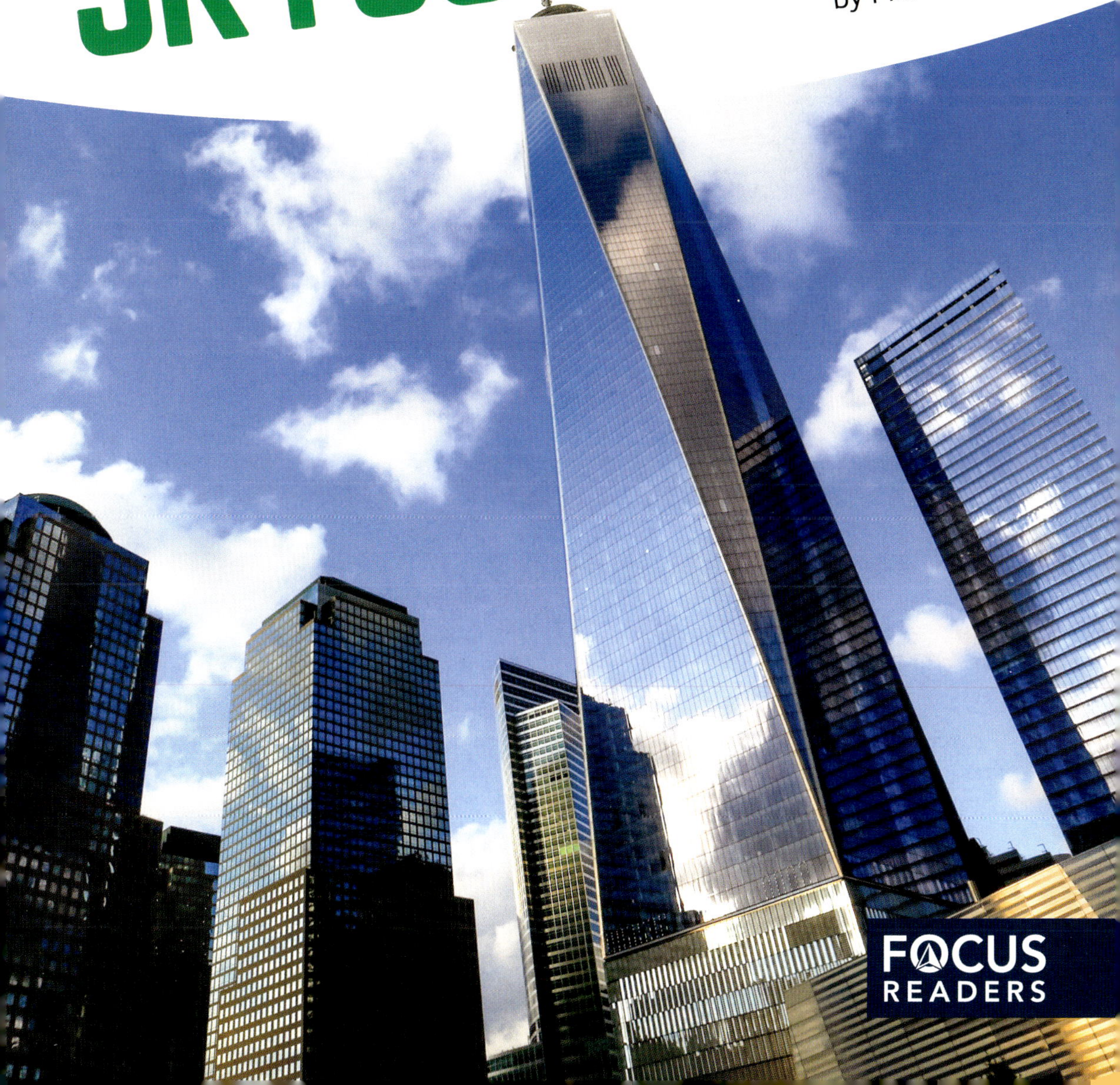

FOCUS READERS

FOCUS READERS

WWW.FOCUSREADERS.COM

Focus Readers is distributed by North Star Editions:
sales@northstareditions.com | 888-417-0195

Produced for Focus Readers by Red Line Editorial.

Content Consultant: Lawrence C. Novak, Senior Director of Structural Engineering & Codes, Portland Cement Association

Photographs ©: batuhanozdel/iStockphoto, cover, 1; Methanon/Shutterstock Images, 4–5; TraceRouda/iStockphoto, 7; ferrantraite/iStockphoto, 9; photo courtesy of Lawrence Novak, 10–11, 13; fazon1/iStockphoto, 14; Songquan Deng/Shutterstock Images, 16; Christopher Penler/Shutterstock Images, 18–19; rabbit75_ist/iStockphoto, 21; dblight/iStockphoto, 22–23; Red Line Editorial, 24–25, 26, 29

ISBN
978-1-63517-256-0 (hardcover)
978-1-63517-321-5 (paperback)
978-1-63517-451-9 (ebook pdf)
978-1-63517-386-4 (hosted ebook)

Library of Congress Control Number: 2017935935

Printed in the United States of America
Mankato, MN
June, 2017

ABOUT THE AUTHOR

Marne Ventura is the author of 48 books for kids. She enjoys writing about science, technology, arts and crafts, and the lives of creative people. A former elementary school teacher, Marne holds a master's degree in education from the University of California. She and her husband live on the central coast of California.

TABLE OF CONTENTS

CHAPTER 1

REACHING FOR THE SKY

The elevator door slid open. Amelia and her friends were 1,354 feet (413 m) in the air. The students walked to the Skydeck. They stood at the top of the Willis Tower in Chicago, Illinois. From the glass structure, Amelia could see parts of four states. People on the sidewalk seemed as tiny as ants.

The Skydeck is on the 103rd floor of the Willis Tower in Chicago.

Builders have been reaching for the sky for ages. Pyramids in ancient Egypt were made of heavy stone. In the Middle Ages, builders used stone to construct churches and towers. These buildings had few windows, so they were cold and dark. And the structures couldn't be built too high. The weight of the stone would cause them to collapse.

Things started to change during the 1700s and 1800s. This period was known as the Industrial Revolution. It was a time when many new machines were being invented. Millions of people were moving away from the country to work in cities.

New York City's Empire State Building was the world's tallest building from 1931 to 1972.

However, this created challenges for engineers. They had to figure out how to fit more homes and offices in the crowded cities. And then they had to make their buildings safe, comfortable, and fireproof.

Inventions such as **steel**, **concrete**, and elevators helped the engineers meet these challenges.

The word *skyscraper* was first used in the 1880s. That was when the Home Insurance Building was built in Chicago. At 10 stories high, it was the world's first skyscraper.

New building materials and designs soon led to taller buildings. The Empire State Building in New York City was completed in 1931. It had more than 100 stories. Today's skyscrapers have many stories for offices or living space. People recognize many cities by their **skylines**.

Skyscrapers allow more people to work and live in a city.

Experts predict that approximately 70 percent of the world's people will live in cities by 2050. Skyscrapers are one solution to fitting more people on less land. They keep cities from spreading outward. And they give each city its own look. Today, engineers are finding new ways to create amazing buildings that reach for the sky.

CHAPTER 2

SKYSCRAPER DESIGN

Skyscrapers must be safe, comfortable places for people to live and work. Engineers take many steps to ensure this. A skyscraper has to resist **forces** called **loads**. The dead load is the weight of the building materials. The live load is the weight of the people and things, such as furniture, inside the skyscraper.

Skyscrapers must be custom built for their setting and needs.

Engineers also consider natural elements. These include wind, fire, and earthquakes. For example, wind blowing against a skyscraper is a strong load. This causes the tower to flex and bend, similar to a tall blade of grass. Earth's gravity is another load. And earthquakes can cause unpredictable loads. A skyscraper needs to be stable and remain standing despite the forces that push against it.

A **foundation** supports a building. Taller buildings have heavier loads, so they need strong, deep foundations. Builders dig down through the upper layers of the soil. Finally, they get to the stable **bedrock** layer. Then they pour

Workers build the foundation at Burj Khalifa in the United Arab Emirates.

concrete over steel bars. This makes the building's foundation. The foundation supports the building and adds stability.

Next, builders construct the frame of the skyscraper on top of the foundation. The frames of early skyscrapers were simple steel boxes with smaller boxes inside. Steel beams supported the weight of the building.

Some of the world's tallest skyscrapers are in Shanghai, China.

Later, designers used a system of frames or walls in the shape of a vertical tube. This allowed engineers to give the skyscrapers more floor space. They didn't need horizontal frames anymore. That meant the buildings were lighter and could be higher.

The vertical tube design also created an inner core. Designers installed elevators here. The lighter core formed a strong backbone. It helped the building resist wind and other forces. It also took the load off of the exterior walls. Since the outer walls were not load-bearing, designers could use materials such as glass on the building's exterior. This let in lots of light. It also looked nice.

Skyscrapers must also be designed for people to use them. People need to be able to move easily up and down the building. The temperature and humidity needs to be comfortable. The building needs electricity. It also needs plumbing.

The Lloyds Building in London, England, is sometimes called the "Inside-Out Building" for its unique design.

The planners must consider the design, too. They want people to be amazed and inspired when they look up at their buildings. An engineer must consider all of these factors when planning a skyscraper.

ENGINEERING DESIGN PROCESS

Engineers use various tools and do many tests in their planning. Once a skyscraper is built, they expect the design to be safe and sturdy.

ASK: Where will the skyscraper be built? What will it be used for? How many people will it need to fit? What materials are available?

IMAGINE: Brainstorm possible skyscraper designs. Think of an idea that is unique but safe.

PLAN: Draw a diagram of the skyscraper. Make a list of the materials needed. Write down the steps that will need to be taken to build it.

CREATE: Follow the plan to build the skyscraper.

IMPROVE: What worked with the skyscraper? What could be improved? How could the design change to make the skyscraper taller?

CHAPTER 3

BUILDING A SKYSCRAPER

Terrorists destroyed the World Trade Center towers in New York City on September 11, 2001. A new tower, One World Trade Center, was to be a memorial to the people who died there. But the new tower also needed to be safe and strong. Planners wanted it to use new technology and be environmentally friendly, too.

Workers build One World Trade Center in New York City.

The building site was in the middle of crowded New York City. Train tracks and subway tracks were already in place. So, engineers had to find a way to lay a strong foundation over these tracks. They designed steel bridges to support the concrete **anchor**. They also used a concrete core and steel frame for the skyscraper. In addition, they designed a shape that would decrease the building's wind load.

One World Trade Center has 70 elevators and a special stairway for fire and safety workers. Parts of the building are made with recycled materials. The glass sides let in sunlight so that less

One World Trade Center towers over the Manhattan skyline.

electricity is needed. Rainwater is used to cool the tower and to water plants.

The height of One World Trade Center is 1,776 feet (541 m). This number was a tribute to the year the United States became a nation. When the building opened in May 2015, it was the tallest skyscraper in the United States. Only three skyscrapers in the world were taller.

BURJ KHALIFA

In January 2010, builders completed work on Burj Khalifa, a skyscraper in Dubai, United Arab Emirates. At 2,717 feet (828 m), it was by far the tallest building in the world. And because of its modern design, Burj Khalifa is half the weight of the Empire State Building. But it is twice as high.

The architects and engineers made the building with a Y-shaped floor plan. This shape is stable. It limits the wind pressure against the building. It also creates good space for living. In addition, this gives people a better view of the Arabian Gulf. Burj Khalifa contains 900 homes, 37 floors of office space, 57 elevators, 8 escalators, and a hotel. It also has five swimming pools.

Burj Khalifa is more than 160 stories tall.

CHAPTER 4

SKYSCRAPER CHALLENGE

Now it's your turn to be an engineer. Build the tallest skyscraper you can. Try to use as few materials as possible to keep the structure light.

Materials:

For this challenge you'll need craft sticks, clothespins, binder clips, and a table to work on.

This sturdy skyscraper model has a strong foundation and is four levels high.

These materials are all you need to build a model skyscraper.

Procedure:

1. Plan a shape for your skyscraper. Do you want the base to be a square or a triangle? What about a rectangle?

2. Begin connecting the wooden craft sticks using the clothespins and binder clips.
3. Continue adding more sticks to go higher and higher. But be sure to test the structure to make sure it can stand on its own.

Considerations:

- Create wind against the side of your skyscraper by blowing or fanning. Does it remain standing?
- Create an earthquake. Place your skyscraper on a piece of cardboard, and slide the cardboard back and forth. Does your skyscraper remain sturdy?

Improve It!

- Can you change the foundation shape to make your skyscraper taller?
- Experiment with different widths, heights, and shapes. How can you use the same materials to make a stronger shape?
- Are there any materials you can remove without affecting the strength of your skyscraper?

This skyscraper model is six levels high and has a unique crown on top.

FOCUS ON
BUILDING SKYSCRAPERS

Write your answers on a separate piece of paper.

1. Write a letter to a friend describing the main idea of Chapter 3.
2. Would you like to live in a skyscraper? Why or why not?
3. Which building was the world's first skyscraper?
    - **A.** Empire State Building
    - **B.** One World Trade Center
    - **C.** Home Insurance Building
4. Why is it helpful to have exterior walls that don't bear any load?
    - **A.** The walls allow more windows.
    - **B.** The walls are heavier.
    - **C.** The walls are straighter.

Answer key on page 32.

GLOSSARY

anchor
A strong support that holds something in place.

bedrock
The layer of solid rock under soil.

concrete
A strong, stone-like material made from gravel, sand, cement, and water.

loads
Masses or weights supported by something.

forces
Pushes or pulls that happen when one object interacts with another object.

foundation
The supporting base of a structure.

skylines
The outlines of cities' tallest buildings against the background of the sky.

steel
A strong metal made with iron, carbon, and other materials.

terrorists
People who use violence to achieve a political goal.

TO LEARN MORE

BOOKS

Beck, Barbara. *The Future Architect's Handbook*. Atglen, PA: Schiffer, 2014.

Cornille, Didier. *Who Built That? Skyscrapers: An Introduction to Skyscrapers and Their Architects*. New York: Princeton Architectural Press, 2014.

Pinto McCarthy, Cecilia. *Engineering One World Trade Center*. Minneapolis: Abdo Publishing, 2017.

NOTE TO EDUCATORS

Visit **www.focusreaders.com** to find lesson plans, activities, links, and other resources related to this title.

INDEX

Answer Key: 1. Answers will vary; **2.** Answers will vary; **3.** C; **4.** A